Garden

Robert Maass

Henry Holt and Company
New York

A garden is a
world in itself, formed
by a gardener's skill
and imagination.

Within a garden, the cycles and rhythms
of life — plant and animal — are clear to see.

There are gardens that shine brilliantly for just a few weeks, while others bloom from early spring to the first frost.

Some gardens harmonize the color and size of their plants and flowers, while others charm by their lack of order. All gardens require care and attention. For gardeners, it is a labor of love.

Once you've chosen a place to plant your garden, you'll then have to decide what to put in it.

Most plants begin as seeds, and many gardeners like to grow *seedlings* indoors to get an early start on the season.

After the soil has been *tilled* it will be ready for planting.

Seeds are planted directly into the soil. You'll need to space them according to how big or bushy the plants will grow.

Vegetables like lettuce are planted early in the season, as they grow best in cooler weather. *Annual* flowers are planted later, when the air and soil temperatures are warmer.

Once plants begin to flower, insects play an important role in *pollination*. Bees and butterflies spread pollen from one plant to another. The pollen fertilizes flowers.

Tomatoes and strawberries are the fruits that grow from their pollinated flowers.

Earthworms also play a valuable role in the garden. They burrow through the ground, and the tiny pathways they make bring water and air to plant roots.

Worms eat organic matter like old leaves. Their waste is good for the soil because it is rich in *nutrients*.

Gardeners fertilize the soil with *compost*, which is made from a mixture of decaying plant materials. Many gardeners have compost piles in their gardens for regular use. Compost helps feed plants, and keeps the ground moist.

A garden will always need regular watering and weeding. Watering keeps plants alive and healthy. Weeding keeps unwanted plants from taking away water, nutrients, and sunlight from your garden plants.

Climbing plants grip whatever is in their path as they grow toward the sun. Gardeners put up trellises, poles, and ropes to help them along.

As the summer heat sets in,
the garden will fill out and come alive.

A carpet of flowers can be thinned out to increase future growth. Now you can bring a little of your garden indoors to brighten your home.

Soon there will be lots to harvest.

As the summer fades and autumn approaches, gardeners clear out and cut back wilting plants and flowers of the past season. *Pruning* and clearing strengthen the plants for next spring's growth.

Now is the time to plant new *bulbs* for next year.

When all the blooms have faded and the last vegetables have been picked, the garden will seem empty. It needs rest to regain its energy for a new growing season. Despite the winter cold and snow, the warm weather will bring it back to life, and so can you.

Glossary

Annual: A plant that goes through its full life cycle—from germination to flowering to dying—in one growing season. Many annual plants bloom continuously throughout the season. A plant that lives for at least three growing seasons, returning annually, is called a *perennial*.

Bulb: A kind of plant stem that stores food from which flowers grow, like tulips or daffodils.

Compost: Decaying plant matter and other organic material used to improve the soil's health and moisture retention.

Nutrient: Any nourishing ingredient that promotes life.

Pollination: The process by which a male plant's pollen is deposited into a female plant in order to produce seeds, fruits, or vegetables.

Prune: To cut back plants, shrubs, or trees in order to promote healthy growth and shape.

Seedling: A very young plant that grows from its germinated seed.

Till: To prepare and condition the soil.

To Lucas and Lily,
who make it all worthwhile

Henry Holt and Company, Inc., *Publishers since 1866*, 115 West 18th Street, New York, New York 10011
Henry Holt is a registered trademark of Henry Holt and Company, Inc.
Published in Canada by Fitzhenry & Whiteside Ltd., 195 Allstate Parkway, Markham, Ontario L3R 4T8.

Library of Congress Cataloging-in-Publication Data
Maass, Robert. Garden / Robert Maass.
Summary: Discusses the beauty and harmony of gardens, the different kinds, and how to care for them.
1. Gardening—Juvenile literature. 2. Gardens—Juvenile literature. [1. Gardening. 2. Gardens.] I. Title.
SB457.M27 1997 635'. 022'2—dc21 97-23425

0-8050-5477-4 First Edition—1998
Designed by Meredith Baldwin

Printed in the United States of America on acid-free paper.∞
10 9 8 7 6 5 4 3 2 1